PIANO • VOCAL • GUITAR

ULTIMATE

CONTEMPORARY CHRISTIAN

• 45 OF THE BEST •

ISBN 0-634-09944-2

HAL•LEONARD®
CORPORATION

7777 W. BLUEMOUND RD. P.O. BOX 13819 MILWAUKEE, WI 53213

Visit Hal Leonard Online at
www.halleonard.com

Piano · Vocal · Guitar
ULTIMATE
CONTEMPORARY CHRISTIAN

• 45 OF THE BEST •

ALL THINGS NEW

Words and Music by
STEVEN CURTIS CHAPMAN

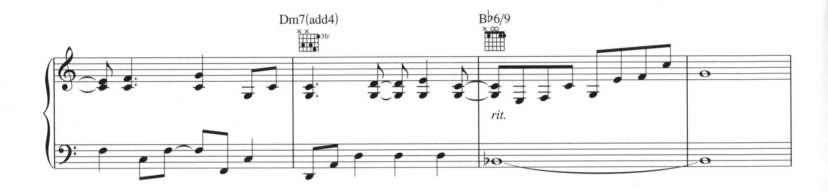

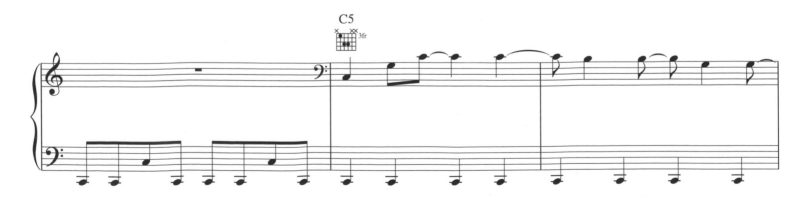

You spoke and made the sun rise to light up the ver - y first day.

You breathed a - cross the wa - ter

Hal - le - lu - jah! ___

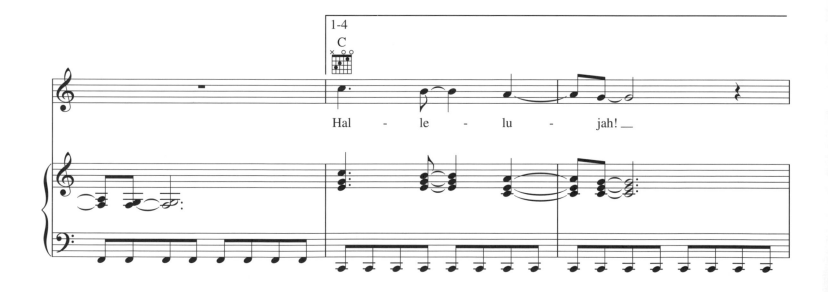

Hal - le - lu - jah! ___

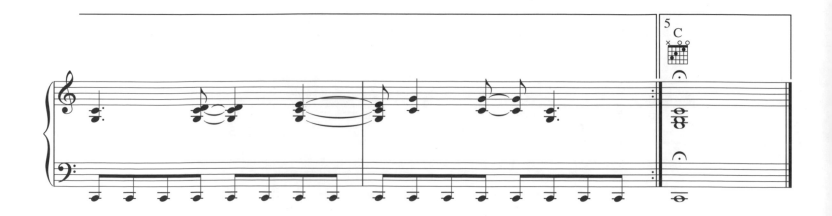

ARISE, MY LOVE

Words and Music by
EDDIE CARSWELL

Slowly, mysteriously

Not a word was heard at the tomb that day, just

shuf-fling sol-diers' feet as they guard-ed the grave. One day, two days,

(Sin), where are your shack - les? (Death), where is your sting?

(Hell) has been de - feat - ed: _____ The grave _____ could not hold _____ our

King.

"A - rise, __

AWESOME GOD

Words and Music by
RICH MULLINS

THE BASICS OF LIFE

Words and Music by MARK HARRIS
and DON KOCH

We've turned the page, _____ for a new day has dawned, _____ and we've re - ar - ranged _____ what is right and what's wrong, _____

CAN'T LIVE A DAY

Words and Music by TY LACY,
CONNIE HARRINGTON and JOE BECK

Bm   A/C♯

- sus, ____ I live __ be - cause __ You live.

D   E

You're like __ the air __ I breathe. __ Oh, _____ Je -

Bm   A/C♯

- sus, _____ Oh, ____ I have __ be - cause __ You gave. _____

D   Esus   N.C.

You're ev - er - y - thing _ to me. __ Oh, __ I could - n't face _

DIVE

Words and Music by
STEVEN CURTIS CHAPMAN

The long a-wait-ed rains _ have fall-en hard _ up-on _ the thirst - y ground; _
There is a su-per-nat-ral pow-er _____ in this might - y riv - er's flow. _

47

Come on, __ let's go. __ I'm div - ing in; I'm go - ing deep,

DYING TO REACH YOU

Words and Music by MICHAEL PURYEAR
and GEOFFREY THURMAN

He looked through tem - ples of time ___
He's stand - ing there at the door; ___

___ to see you right where you ___ stand.
___ you can hear Him call you by name. ___

He emp - tied all of Him - self
He sim - ply waits to for - give

52

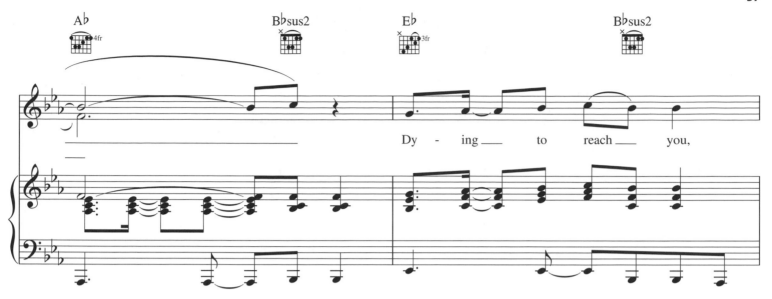

Dy - ing ___ to reach ___ you,

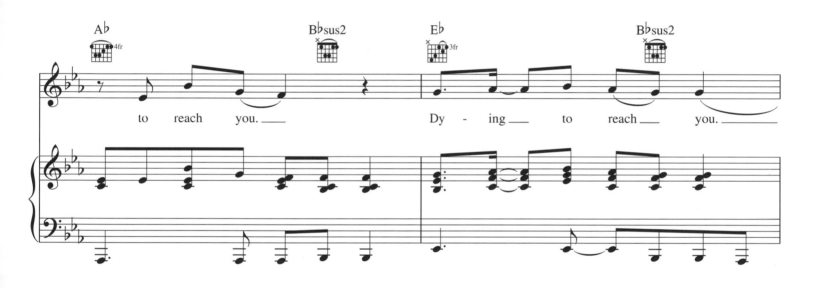

to reach you. ___ Dy - ing ___ to reach ___ you. ___

EL SHADDAI

Words and Music by MICHAEL CARD
and JOHN THOMPSON

EVERYTHING TO ME

Words and Music by SUE SMITH
and CHAD CATES

Male: I grew up___ in Sun - day School;___ I mem - o - rized___ the Gold - en Rule___ and how

Je - sus came___ to set the sin - ner free.___ I

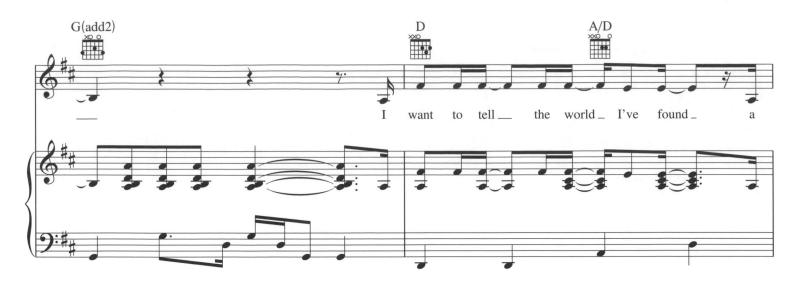

I want to tell __ the world __ I've found __ a

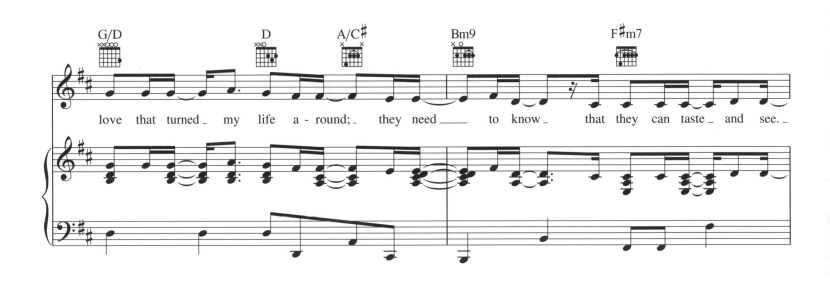

love that turned __ my life a - round; __ they need ____ to know __ that they can taste __ and see. __

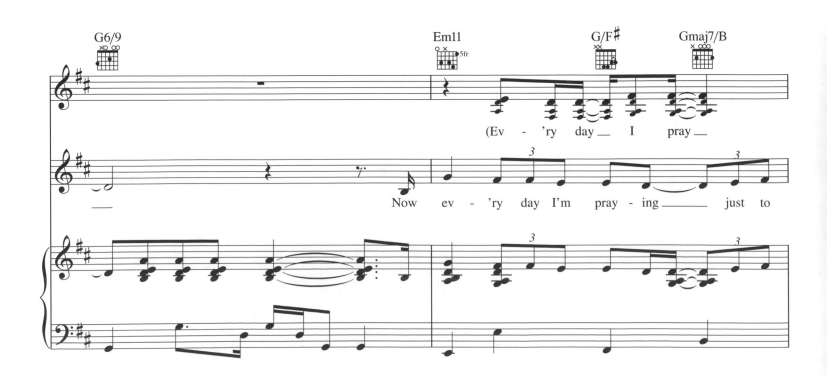

(Ev - 'ry day __ I pray __

Now ev - 'ry day I'm pray - ing ____ just to

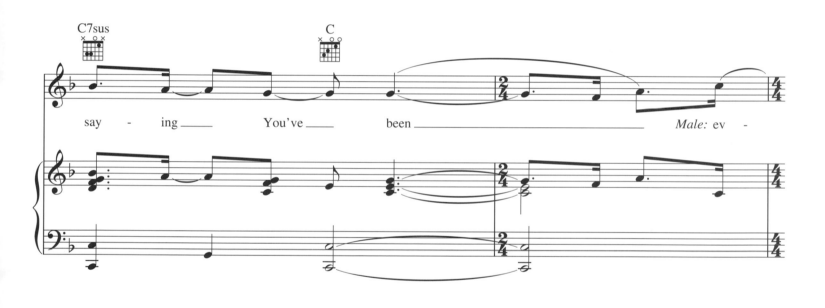

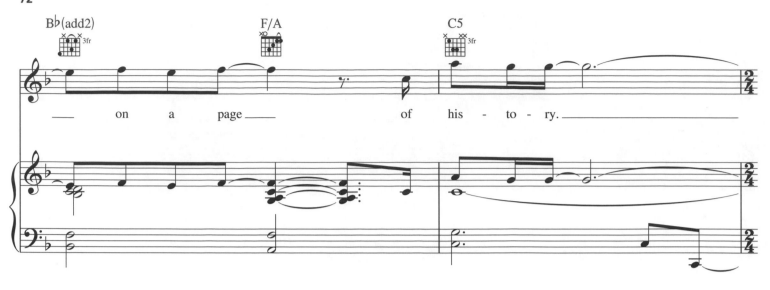

on a page _____ of his-to-ry. _____

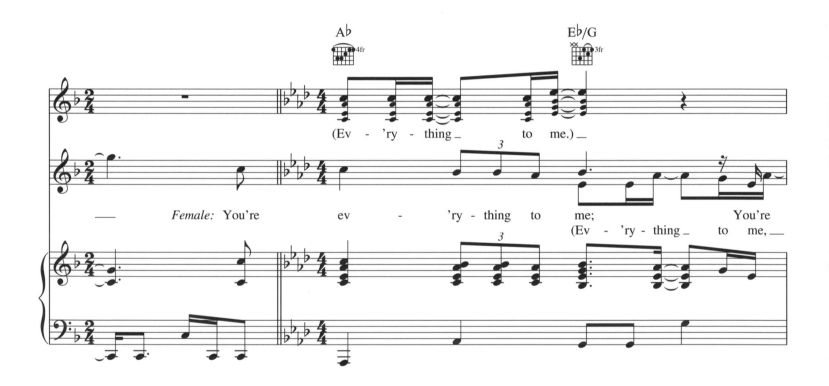

(Ev - 'ry - thing ___ to me.) ___

Female: You're ev - 'ry - thing to me; You're
(Ev - 'ry - thing ___ to me, ___

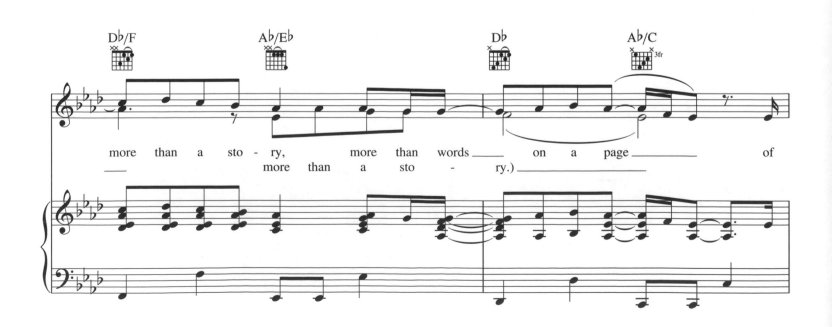

more than a sto - ry, more than words _____ on a page _____ of
___ more than a sto - ry.) _____

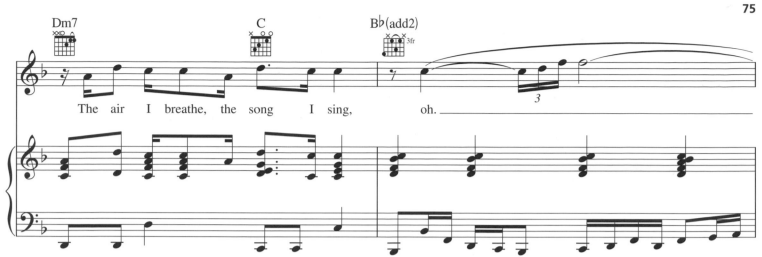

The air I breathe, the song I sing, oh. _____

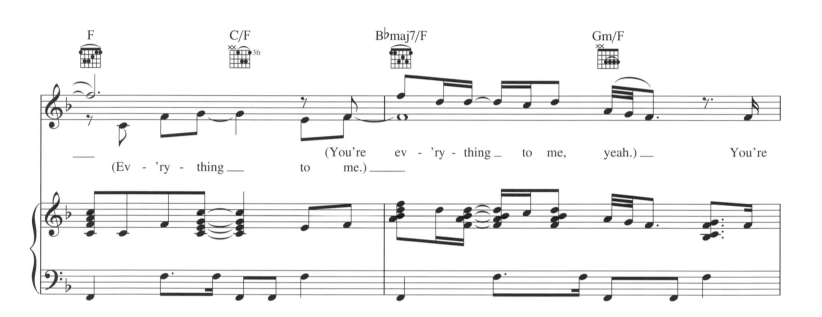

_____ (Ev - 'ry - thing _____ to me.) _____ (You're ev - 'ry - thing _____ to me, yeah.) _____ You're

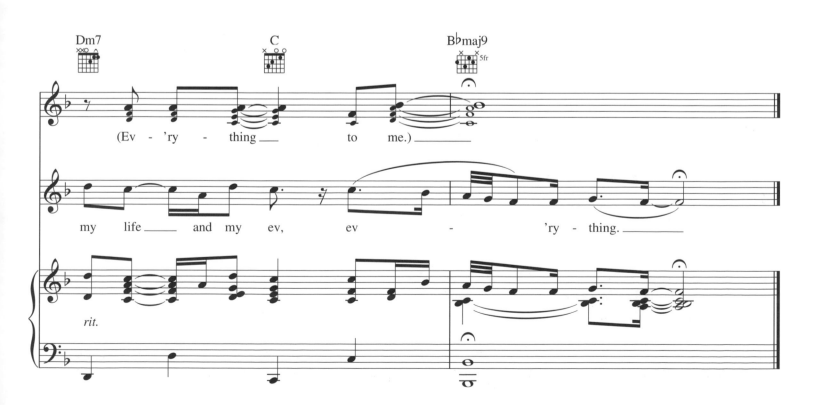

(Ev - 'ry - thing _____ to me.) _____ my life _____ and my ev, ev - 'ry - thing. _____

rit.

FINGERPRINTS OF GOD

Words and Music by
STEVEN CURTIS CHAPMAN

I can see the tears _____ fill-ing your eyes_
been _____ and nev-er a-gain_

_____ and I know where they're_ com - ing _____ from.
_____ will there be an-oth-er_ you,

They're com-ing from a
fash-ioned by God's

FRIENDS

Words and Music by MICHAEL W. SMITH
and DEBORAH D. SMITH

FLOOD

Words and Music by CHARLIE LOWELL, DAN HASELTINE,
MATT ODMARK and STEPHEN MASON

Rain, rain on my face.
Down - pour on my soul.

Has - n't stopped raining for days.
Splash - ing in the o - cean, I'm los - ing con - trol.

GIVE IT UP

Words and Music by RIKK KITTLEMAN,
MICHAEL PASSONS, GRANT CUNNINGHAM,
MARK HEIMERMANN and JANNA POTTER

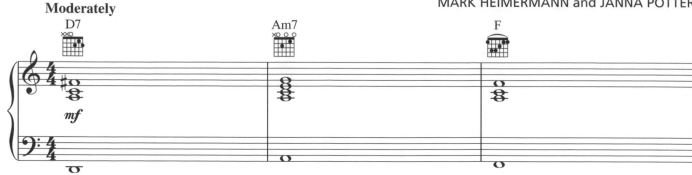

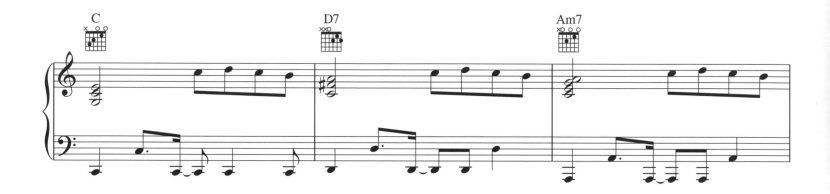

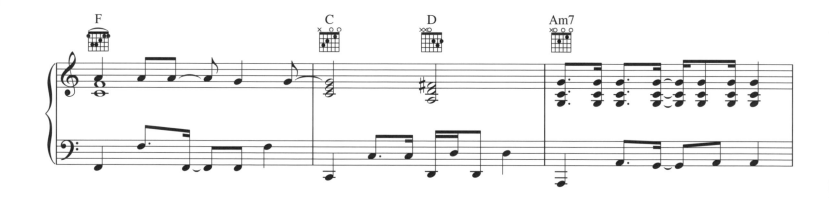

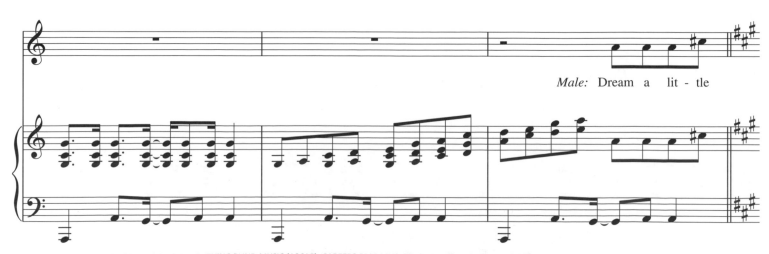

Male: Dream a lit - tle

*Female I lead vocal is written one octave above sounding pitch.

all of your heart (give it up, give it up). Give Him all of your life (give it
(All of your

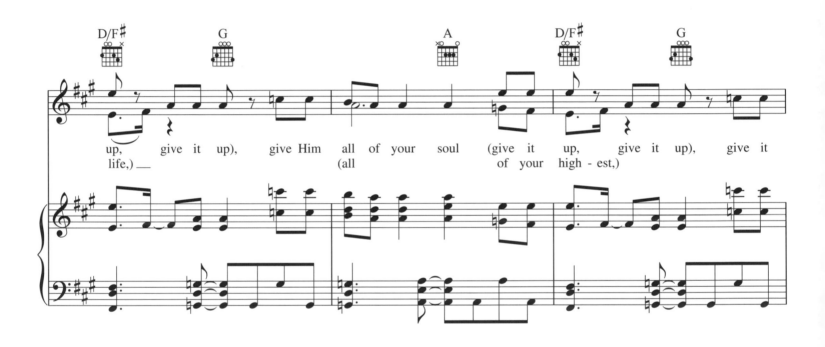

up, give it up), give Him all of your soul (give it up, give it up), give it
life,) ___ (all of your high - est,)

up, give it up (give it up, give it up). Give it up, give it up, whoa. ___
(all of your life.) ____

GO AND SIN NO MORE

Words and Music by REBECCA ST. JAMES,
TEDD TJORNHOM and MICHAEL ANDERSON

GO LIGHT YOUR WORLD

Words and Music by
CHRIS RICE

blaz - ing, so let's raise our can - dles and light up the sky.___

_____ Pray - ing to our Fa - ther,___ in the name___ of Je -

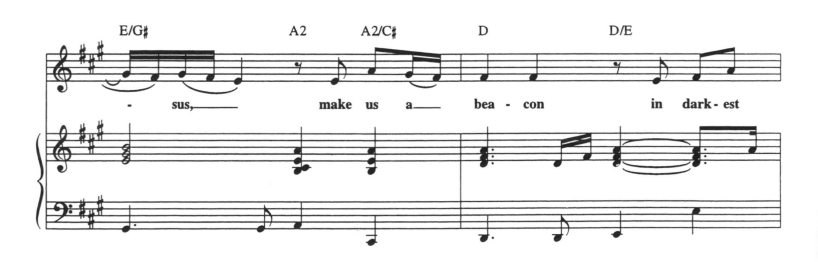

- sus,___ make us a___ bea - con in dark - est

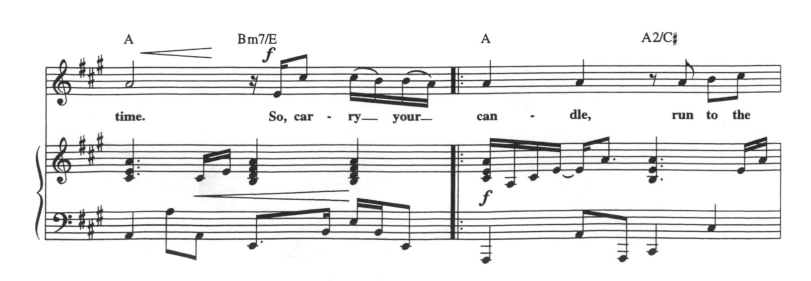

time. So, car - ry___ your___ can - dle, run to the

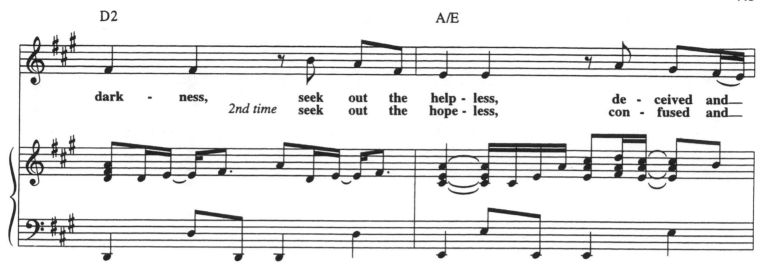

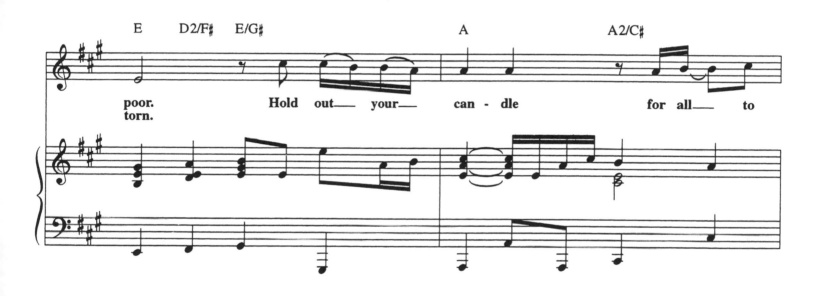

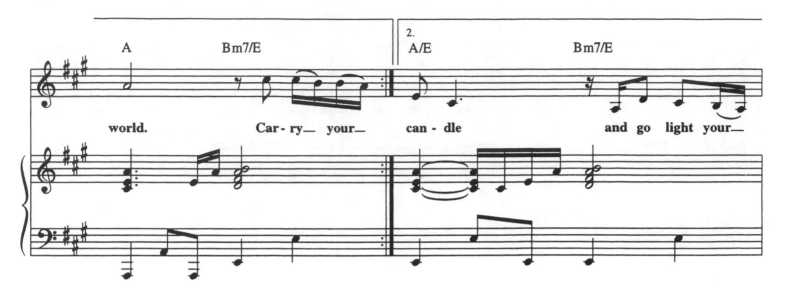

world.   Car - ry___ your___ can - dle   and go light your___

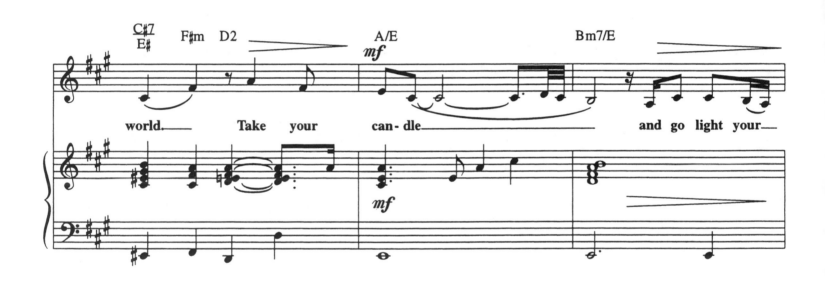

world.___   Take   your   can - dle_____   and go light your___

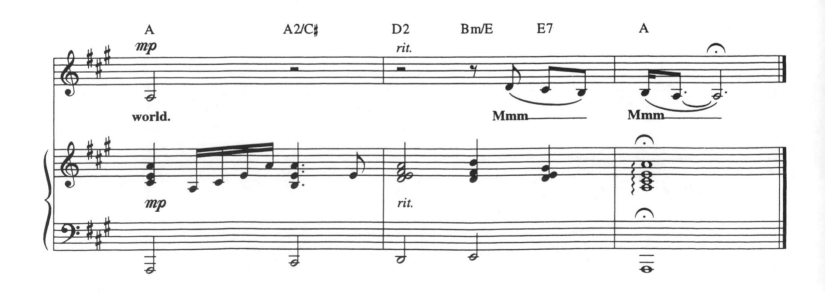

world.   Mmm___   Mmm

THE GREAT ADVENTURE

Words and Music by STEVEN CURTIS CHAPMAN
and GEOFF MOORE

GOD IS IN CONTROL

Words and Music by
TWILA PARIS

This is __ no time for fear. This is __ a time for __ faith and de - ter - min - a - tion.
His - to - ry march - es on. There is __ a bot - tom line drawn a - cross the __ a - ges.

THE GREAT DIVIDE

Words and Music by MATT HUESMANN
and GRANT CUNNINGHAM

HERE I AM

Words and Music by REBECCA ST. JAMES,
BILL DEATON and ERIC CHAMPION

HERE WITH ME

Words and Music by BRAD RUSSELL, BART MILLARD,
MICHAEL SCHEUCHZER, JAMES BRYSON,
ROBIN SHAFFER, NATHAN COCHRAN, BARRY GRAUL,
DAN MUCKALA and PETE KIPLEY

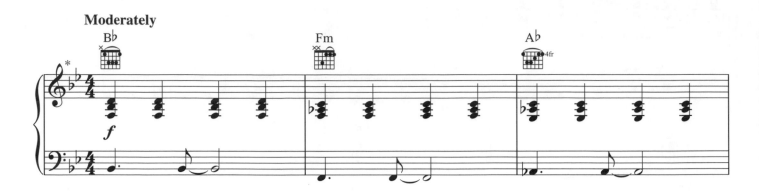

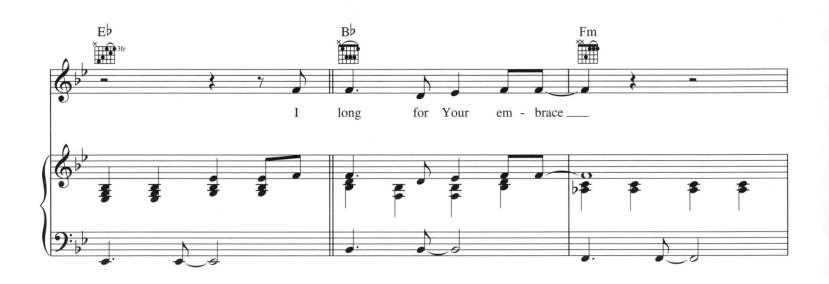

I long for Your em-brace

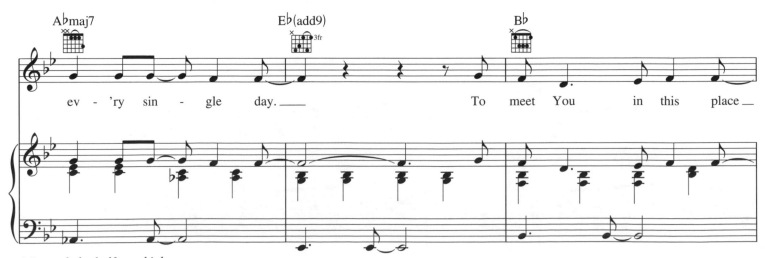

ev-'ry sin-gle day. To meet You in this place

* Recorded a half step higher.

148

- ment I ___ sur - ren - der to ___ Your ___ love. ___

HIS STRENGTH IS PERFECT

Words and Music by STEVEN CURTIS CHAPMAN
and JERRY SALLEY

HOLY

Words and Music by NICHOLE NORDEMAN
and MARK HAMMOND

I CAN ONLY IMAGINE

Words and Music by
BART MILLARD

I SURRENDER ALL

Words and Music by DAVID MOFFITT
and REGIE HAMM

wres - tled in __ the dark - ness of this lone - ly pil - grim land, __ rais - ing
source of my __ am - bi - tion is the treas - ure I __ ob - tain, __ if I

strong and might - y for - tress - es __ that I a - lone com - mand, __ but these
meas - ure my __ suc - cess - es __ on a scale __ of earth - ly gain, __ if the

D

cas - tles I've _ con - struct - ed by the strength of my _ own hand _ are just
fo - cus of _ my _ vi - sion is the stat - us I _____ at - tain, _ my ac -

F#

Bm

tem - po - ra - ry king - doms on _ foun - da - tions made _ of sand. _ In the
com - plish - ments _ are worth - less and my ef - forts are _ in vain. _ So I

Asus

D/F#

G(add2)

mid - dle of _ the bat - tle I be - lieve I've fi - n'lly found _ I'll nev - er
lay a - side _ these tro - phies to pur - sue a high - er crown, _ and should You

D/F#

G(add2)

know the thrill _ of vic - t'ry till I'm _ will - ing to _ lay down _ all my
choose some - how _ to use _ the life _ I will - ing - ly _ lay down, _ I sur -

D

D/F#

fall, _____ that all my king - doms fall, let all ___ my king - doms ___

___ fall, _____ I sur - ren - der

all. _____

I STILL BELIEVE

Words and Music by
JEREMY CAMP

E - ven when I don't see, ____

____ I still be - lieve. ____

JOY

Words and Music by PETER FURLER
and STEVE TAYLOR

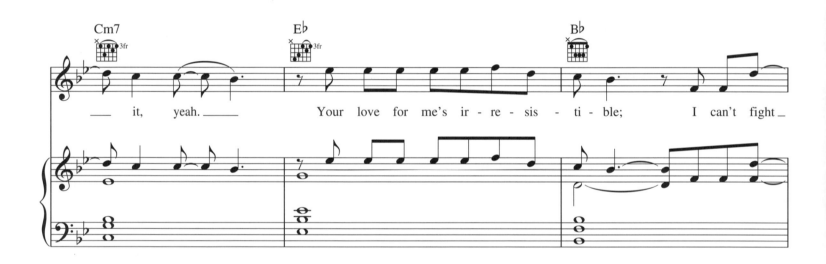

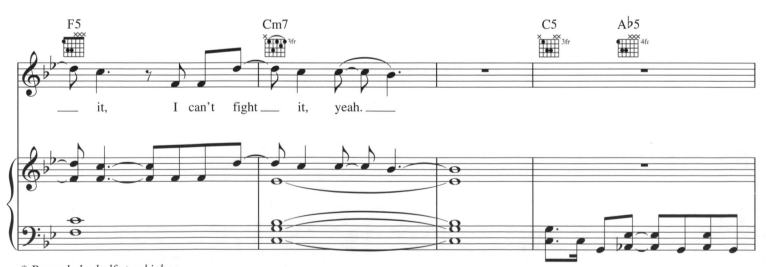

Recorded a half step higher.

MORE

Words and Music by KENNY GREENBERG,
JASON HOUSER and MATTHEW WEST

MERCY CAME RUNNING

Words and Music by DAN DEAN,
DAVE CLARK and DON KOCH

Once there was a ho - ly__ place,__
Once there was a bro - ken__ heart,__

ev - i - dence__ of God's em - brace;__
way too hu - man from the__ start;__

MY FAITH WILL STAY

Words and Music by
CHERI KEAGGY

MY LIFE IS IN YOUR HANDS

Words and Music by KATHY TROCCOLI
and BILL MONTVILO

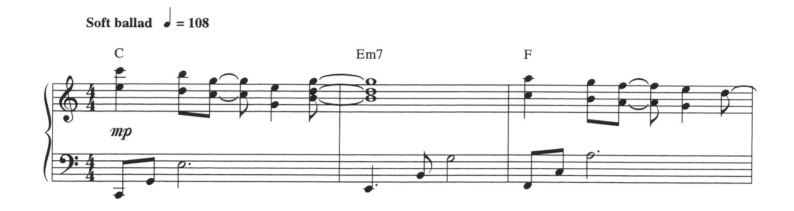

1. Life can be___ so good,___ life can be___ so hard,___
2. Noth-ing is___ for sure, noth-ing is___ for keeps.

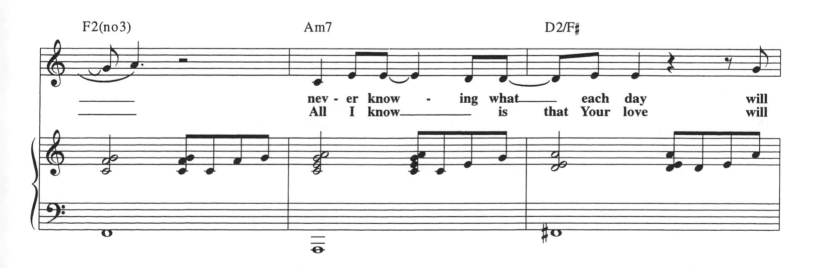

nev - er know - ing what___ each day will
All I know___ is that Your love will

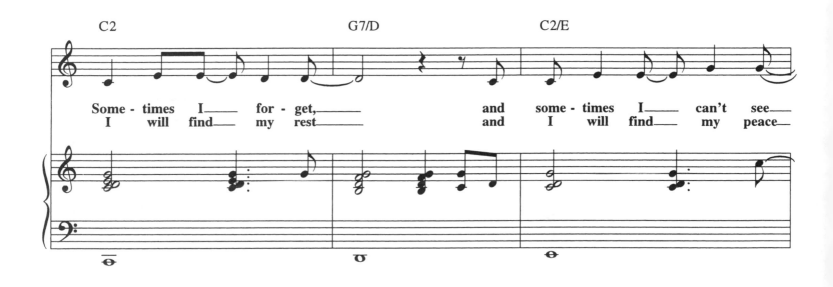

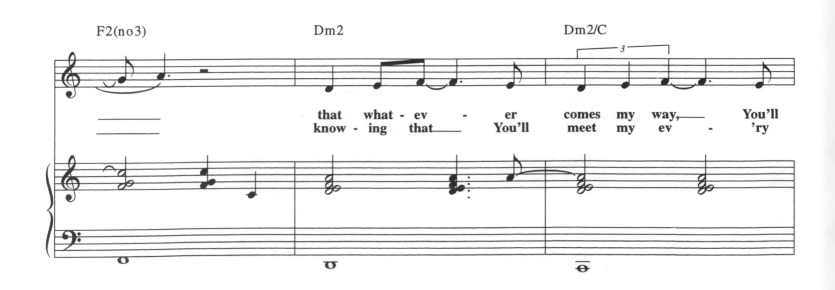

ONE OF THESE DAYS

Words and Music by
JEROMY DEIBLER

PLACE IN THIS WORLD

Words by WAYNE KIRKPATRICK and AMY GRANT
Music by MICHAEL W. SMITH

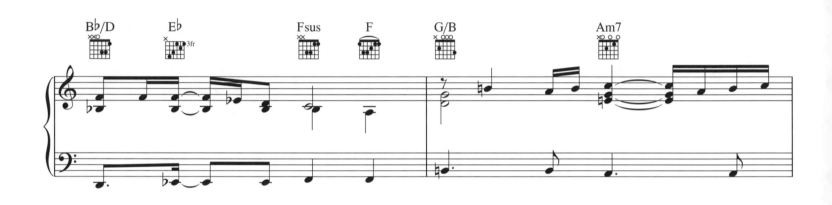

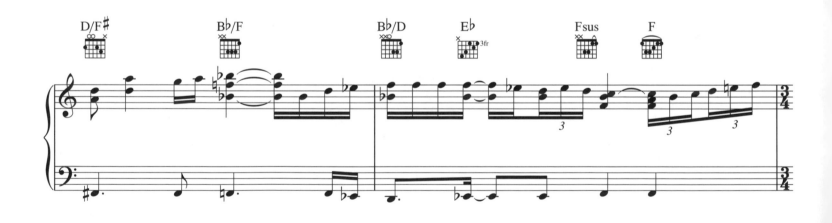

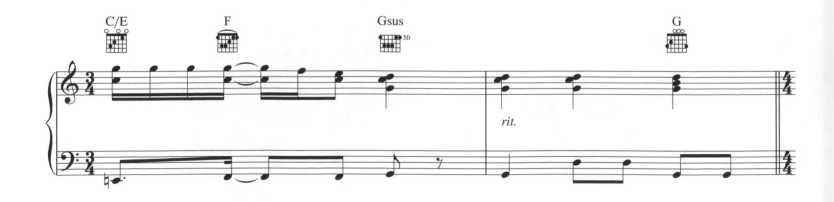

SHINE

Words and Music by PETER FURLER
and STEVE TAYLOR

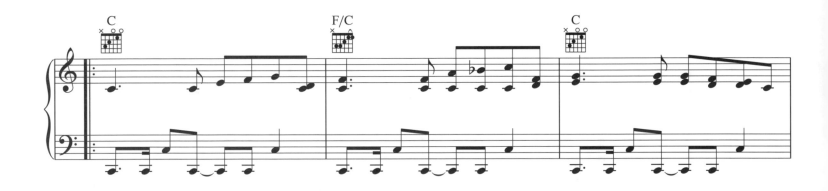

Dull as dirt,____ you can't as - sert the kind of light____
Out of the shak - er and on - to the plate, it is - n't Kar -

SHINE ON US

Words and Music by MICHAEL W. SMITH
and DEBBIE SMITH

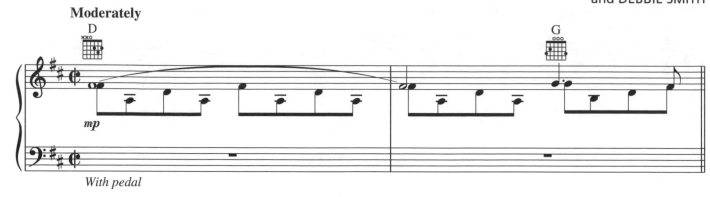

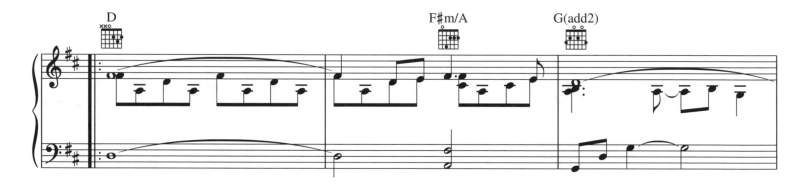

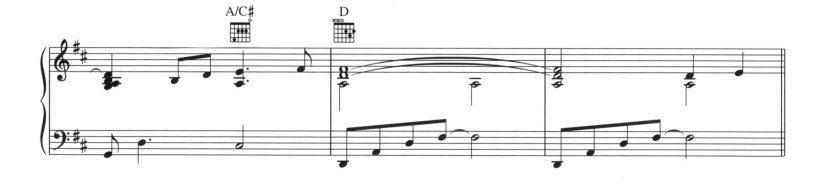

Lord, _____ let your light,
Lord, _____ let your grace,

STEADY ON

Words and Music by GRANT CUNNINGHAM
and MATT HUESMANN

Kick-in' up dust, heav-en or bust, we're head-ed for the prom-ised land.__ Since the mo -
wan-na walk a while; we know__ that ev-'ry mile is bring-ing us clos-er home.__ We wan -

-ment we be - lieved we've been ea - ger to leave, __ like a child tug-gin' Dad-dy's hand. May we
-na tell the sto - ry of sin-ners bound for glo - ry and turn to find we're not a - lone. When we

nev - er for - get that pa - tience is a vir - tue. __ Calm our
walk in Your light, the lost will see You bet - ter. __ As the

an - xious feet so faith - ful hands __ can __ serve You, Lord. __ } We
nar - row road gets crowd - ed, Lord, __ won't You lead us stead-y on? __ }

run on up __ a - head, __ we lag be - hind You. It's

THIS IS HOW IT FEELS TO BE FREE

Words and Music by SHAWN CRAIG,
DAVE CLARK and DON KOCH

Speak-in' as ___ a pris-'ner who was there and lived ___ to tell, I re-
though my heart ___ was will-in', I just stood there at ___ the wall, pray-in'
feel the voice ___ of e-vil, I can hear the call ___ of sin, but I

mem-ber how it felt. I could
some-how it would fall. But in a
won't go back a-gain. See, ___

cross I found the door-way in a hand that held the keys. ___
once I tast-ed free-dom, then the walls could bind no more. ___ Since

When the chains ___ fell at my feet, for the first time, I could see. ___
mer-cy gave ___ me wings to fly, like an ea-gle, I can soar. ___

THIS IS YOUR TIME

Words and Music by MICHAEL W. SMITH
and WES KING

With conviction ♩. = 55

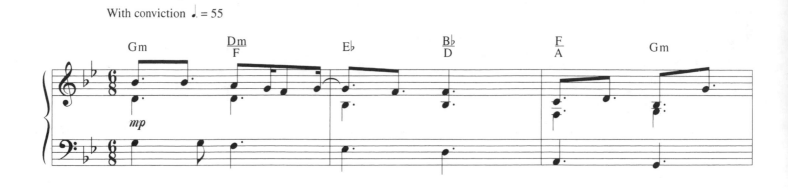

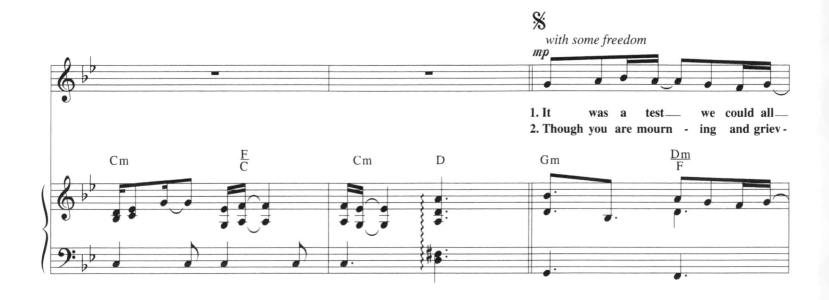

1. It was a test__ we could all
2. Though you are mourn - ing and griev -

__ hope to pass,__ but none of us would__ want__ to take.__
- ing your loss,__ death died a long__ time__ a - go.__

Faced with the choice to de - ny God and live, for
Swal - lowed in life, so her life car - ries on,

her there was one choice to make.
still, it's so hard to let go. } This was her time,

this was her dance, she lived ev - 'ry mo - ment, left noth - in' to

chance. She swam in the sea, drank of the deep, em - braced the mys -

2nd time to Coda

-ter-y of all___ she could be;___

Gm7   Eb2   Eb

This was her time.___

Gm   F   Eb   Bb/D

D.S. al CODA 𝄋

F/A   Gm   Cm   F/C   Cm   D

⊕ *CODA*

-ter-y of all___ she could be.   What if to-mor-

Gm7   Eb2   Eb

save_____ me?"

This is your time,_____ this is your dance,_____ live ev - 'ry mo -

- ment, leave noth - in'_____ to chance. Swim in the sea,_____ drink of the deep,_____

1.

em - brace the mys - ter - y_____ of all you can be._____ This is your time,_____

THY WORD

Words and Music by MICHAEL W. SMITH
and AMY GRANT

Noth - ing will __ I __ fear as __ long as You __ are __ near.

Please be near me to the end. __

Thy Word is a lamp __ un-to __ my feet __ and a __

light __ un-to __ my path.

TO KNOW YOU

Words and Music by NICHOLE NORDEMAN
and MARK HAMMOND

Moderately slow

It's well past mid-night and I'm a-wake with ques-tions that won't wait for day-light, sep-a-rat-ing fact from my i-mag- i-nar-y fic-tion on this shelf of my con-vic-tion. I

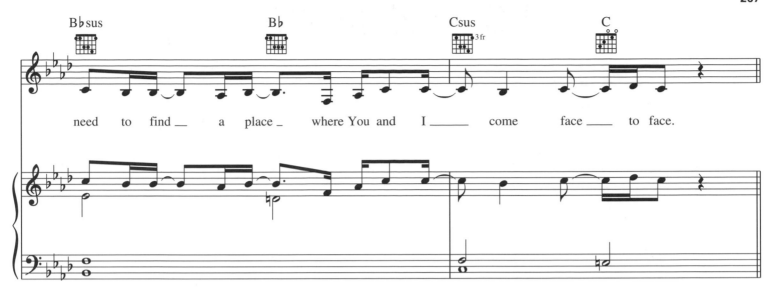

need to find __ a place __ where You and I ____ come face ____ to face.

Thom - as need - ed proof that You __ had real - ly ris - en
Nic - o - de - mus could not un - der - stand __ how You could

un - de - feat - ed. When he placed __ his fin - gers where the
tru - ly free __ us. He strug - gled with __ the im - age of a

nails once _ broke Your skin, _ did his faith fi - n'lly be - gin? _____ I've
grown man _ born a - gain. _ We might have been good friends, _ cuz

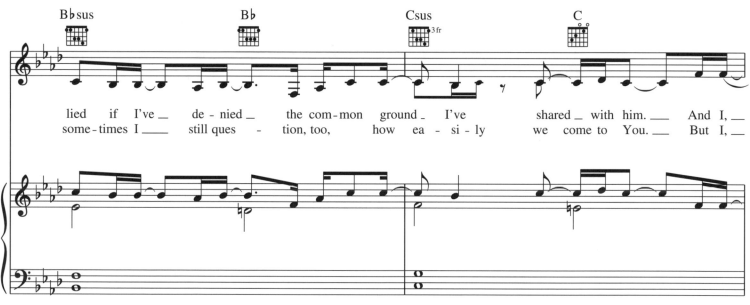

lied if I've _ de - nied _ the com-mon ground _ I've shared _ with him. ___ And I, _
some-times I ____ still ques - tion, too, how ea - si - ly we come to You. ___ But I, _

I real - ly want _ to know _ You. I

UNDO ME

Words and Music by
JENNIFER KNAPP

Pa - pa, ___ I think I messed up a - gain. ___ Was it some-thin' I did or was it some-

- thin' I ___ said? ___ I don't mean ___ to do ___ you wrong; it's just the way ___

___ of hu - man na - ture. Sis - ter, ___ I know I

let you down; ___ I can tell by the fact you'll nev - er come a - round. ___

You don't ___ have to say ___ a thing; ___ I can tell ___

___ by your eyes ___ ex - act - ly what you mean: ___ that it's time ___ to get down ___

___ on my knees ___ and pray, ___ "Lord, un - do ___ me.

VOICE OF TRUTH

Words and Music by MARK HALL
and STEVEN CURTIS CHAPMAN

Oh what I ___ would do ___ to have ___ the kind of faith ___ it takes ___ to climb out ___ of this boat I'm in, ___

WHERE THERE IS FAITH

Words and Music by
BILLY SIMON

I be-lieve __ in faith-ful-ness, __
There's a man __ a-cross __ the sea __

I be-lieve __ in giv-ing of __ my- self __
nev-er heard __ the sound __ of free-dom ring, __

for some- one _____ else. _____
on - ly __ in _____ his _____ dreams. _

WHO AM I

Words and Music by
MARK HALL

Recorded a half step higher.

303

WORD OF GOD SPEAK

Words and Music by BART MILLARD
and PETE KIPLEY

WISDOM

Words and Music by
TWILA PARIS

I see a mul - ti - tude _ of peo - ple,
There is a mo - ment of __ de - ci - sion,